Bygone Brechin
John Alexander

Brechin's City Bell Ringers photographed about 1910.

© John Alexander, 2024
First published in the United Kingdom, 2024,
by Stenlake Publishing Ltd.
www.stenlake.co.uk
ISBN 978-1-84033-968-0

The publishers regret that they cannot supply
copies of any pictures featured in this book.

Printed by
P2D Books, 1 Newlands Rd, Westoning, Bedford, MK45 5LD

Further Reading

The following were the principal books and websites used by the author during his research. None are available from Stenlake Publishing; please contact your local bookshop, reference library or search for them on the internet.

Barnard, Alfred, *The Whisky Distilleries of the United Kingdom*, 1887.
Black, David, D. *The History of Brechin to 1864*, 1867.
Centenary Souvenir of Brechin United Co-operative Society 1833-1933.
Cornwell, H. J. C., *Forty Years of Caledonian Locomotives*, 1882-1922, 1974.
Gifford, John, *The Buildings of Scotland, Dundee and Angus*, 2012.
Henderson, I. A. N., *Discovering Angus & The Mearns*, 1990.
MacGibbon, David, & Ross, Thomas, *The Ecclesiastical Architecture of Scotland*, 1896.
Thomas, John, & Turnock, David, *A Regional History of the Railways of Great Britain, Vol. 15 North of Scotland*, 1989.

Websites
As well as subject-specific sites some general ones were also searched, namely: British Newspaper Archive, Canmore, Dictionary of Scottish Architects, Electric Scotland and NLS Maps.

Brechin photographers cashed in on scenes of major weather events, like this snowstorm that hit the town in January 1907.

Introduction

The Picts, those ancient enigmatic people who occupied all of eastern Scotland north of the Forth including the area now called Angus, left no written records so although they almost certainly lived in and around Brechin, to what extent is not known. It is the church therefore that provides the first documentary evidence for a settlement. Established before the year 1,000 that early religious site developed into a place of some significance, a Bishopric with a cathedral. Secular power also put down roots with an adjacent castle that became the focus of fighting and feuding. Here, in 1296, the putative Scottish King, John Baliol, suffered the humiliation of having to surrender the country's crown and seal to Edward I of England, and seven years later Edward was back to burnish his reputation as 'hammer of the Scots', and hammer the castle into submission.

Time moved on from that medieval turbulence, Brechin became a Royal Burgh, which meant it could tax, trade and hold markets, so the cathedral city became a market town, drawing on the produce of a large, rich agricultural hinterland. Changes wrought on that rural landscape in the 18th century saw large numbers of people leave the land and move into villages and larger towns, like Brechin. Many began to earn a living by weaving linen cloth on handlooms in their own houses using yarn derived from locally grown flax. Trade expanded, and demand grew to soon outstrip supply, and so flax had to be imported in large quantities from Russia and northern Europe, and because it came into east coast ports, linen weaving in Angus became a large and important industry. Brechin was at the forefront. Spinning mills to process the raw flax were established and large bleach fields set up beside the River South Esk. Weavers moved off their home-based looms to work in large handloom factories and when power looms were invented these same factories quickly started to use them, thus completing Brechin's transition to an industrial town. Other industries established were based on serving the needs of agriculture or using its produce like barley for distilling whisky.

Industrial growth led to expansion of the town with new streets, churches, housing, extensive parks and some fine civic buildings like the imposing Mechanics Institute. Industry also created a need for better transport, but in the early days of railways Brechin was initially by-passed before becoming a minor hub. Roads too were improved in the 19th century, initially as toll roads. These were later taken over by public authorities although the main north-south route still ran through Brechin until the A90 by-pass was made in the second half of the 20th century.

The 20th century also brought another wave of change with closure of the weaving industry and the rise of modern enterprises. And although the cathedral became a parish church some time ago and the bishop moved to Dundee, Brechin is finding ways to value the best from its past, honour local heroes and carve out a role in modern tourism.

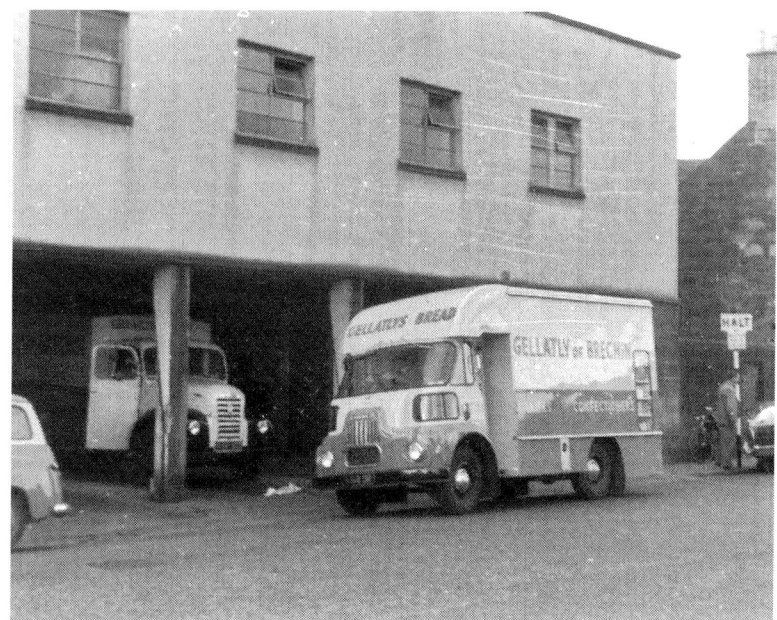

These delivery vans belonging to Gellatly's bakers and confectioners, one of Brechin's longest-lasting businesses, were photographed in 1963.

Situated to the south-west of Brechin, Stannochy is the location of a big house, farm and mill with a large dam that occupies the foreground of this picture. It is also the site of the Stannochy Bridge, which carries the road from Forfar, the modern B9134, over the River South Esk, superseding an earlier ford. It is a very impressive structure, one of the longest single masonry arches in Scotland with a span of 100 feet. Erected in 1826 by James Smith, it bears similarities to other bridges in this part of Angus and the engineer Robert Stevenson may have had an influence on the design. The South Esk has certainly had a major influence on the story of Brechin.

The road into the town from the west, the modern A935, was formerly part of the main road through Strathmore before it was remade as a fast dual carriageway. Prior to that it was a turnpike, or toll road that operated between 1794 and 1879. Such roads were made by companies authorised by Act of Parliament to build and maintain roads and to collect tolls to cover their costs. This was done at toll bars or gates attached to cottages with windows that gave the toll keeper good sight of the road, like the one seen here known as the West Toll. The horses and carts are standing next to the junction with the road to and from Stannochy on the right.

To the east of the West Toll the road in and out of town is named Castle Street, which is a pretty big clue as to what lies in the vicinity. The street is seen here looking back to the west with distant trees on the left marking the location of the ornate gateway to the castle. The trees in the right distance indicate the equally ornate entry to Bearehill, a late Georgian villa that was home to one of the linen mill owners. Somewhat modified around 1870, it was more recently adapted for use as a care home. In the right foreground, adjacent to the entrance for another large villa, is the southern end of Conveners Wynd, formerly known as Western Lane.

Intent on going down in Scottish history as a villain, Edward I besieged and captured Brechin Castle in 1303. Just over 200 years later, James V granted the castle and lands to Thomas Erskine. In 1634 Patrick Maule of Panmure, who later became the first Earl of Panmure, bought the estate. Following the death of the sixth Earl in 1782, the estate passed to his nephew, the eighth Earl of Dalhousie and five years later to his second son who began a process of reconstruction. That continued through subsequent generations until the early 20th century by which time the structure, as seen in this picture, looked more like a stately home than a fortress that could withstand a medieval siege.

A religious community existed at Brechin before the church was established on the Irish model about the beginning of the 11th century. The most compelling link to Irish influence is the remarkable round tower. Monks are thought to have built such towers as places of refuge from Viking raids, and while familiar in Ireland, only two examples exist in mainland Scotland. Construction of the main cathedral building appears to have begun in the early 13th century and continued through to completion of the square tower, on the opposite corner to the round tower, in the mid to late 14th century.

Following the Reformation some parts of the cathedral were abandoned, or altered to suit the strict new form of worship. Further modifications to the structure took place in the early 19th century, but a hundred years later work was undertaken to revive the medieval character of the building, which succeeded admirably as this interior picture shows.

Running between the cathedral and High Street is Bishop's Close. Old walls built into the pend at the mouth of the close are thought to have been part of the surrounds of the former bishop's palace. That had long gone by the early 20th century and been replaced by the glorious jumble of structures shown in this picture.

As the name implies High Street was the spine of the town with lesser thoroughfares like Bishop's Close branching off. It slopes steeply from north to south and is far from straight, a feature exaggerated by an irregular building line that is more pronounced at the lower southern end, as is evident in this picture looking north. Prominent on the right is Norman Anderson's Stationery Warehouse, a successor to the Bazaar run by D. B. Mackie who traded in a similar range of merchandise. On the uphill side of the shop, J. T. Robertson was a draper while the striped pole on the right hand edge of the picture denotes J. Smith's barber's business.

The gap site in the foreground of this mid-20th century picture has since been utilised as an access point for the Skinners Burn walkway. Opposite is the chunky frontage to the King's Cinema, built in 1926 and a centre of popular entertainment for many years thereafter. It replaced earlier buildings, but by good fortune some of High Street's older buildings survived into an era that saw value in historical structures. Further up the street, but out of picture on the left is a former merchant's house that had become seriously dilapidated before a campaign was mounted to save it. That succeeded and with date stones for 1575 and 2012 mounted on the facade to mark its original construction and restoration, the house is a remarkable survival.

The symbol of Brechin's market town status, the 'mercat' cross, formerly stood at the broad intersection of High Street and Church Street. It had been taken down before 1789 when the Town House, seen here on the left, was built with its distinctive first floor window and birdcage bellcote. As its days of civic importance slipped into history, the upper building was used for a variety of purposes, while the ground floor was occupied by William Low's grocery store and more recently a museum. Some fine buildings facing the Town House with their gable ends fronting the street can be seen very obliquely on the right of the picture. In the foreground of these is Stratton's tobacconist's shop and a couple of doors higher up the street, Walter Hutton's baker's shop and City Restaurant where customers could avail themselves of 'Real Forfar Bridies and Pies'.

The section of High Street shown on the facing page is replicated in this picture, but looking from the opposite direction, downhill from the intersection with St. David and Swan Streets. When the picture was taken in 1922, the shop on the left, No. 1 High Street, was occupied by the licensed grocery store of Robert Hampton having previously been a similar business run by W. Duncan & Co. The neighbouring shop at No. 3 was a drapery run by James Jarron. Facing these shops on the other side of High Street is a large building with a plaque mounted at first floor level that denotes it as the birthplace, in 1803, of Thomas Guthrie D.D. a notable preacher, philanthropist and supporter of the Free Church of Scotland. A larger plaque at a lower level commemorates the centenary of Brechin's co-operative societies.

A co-operative society formed in 1833 opened its first shop at the top of Witchden Road. A second society was set up about ten years later and both operated on the basis of paying equal dividends to all members. At about the same time, in England, the Rochdale Equitable Pioneers Society was set up on the principal of dividends being paid on purchases, rather than just membership. The idea spread and in 1861 was adopted by a new society, the Brechin Equitable. It prospered and bought the premises on the corner of High Street and St. David Street in 1870. Seen here on the left, it was a large store principally used to retail drapery, but also groceries. The two societies amalgamated in 1913 as the Brechin United Co-operative Society, adopted the Rochdale principles and celebrated their combined centenary in 1933.

Just creeping into the right-hand edge of this picture looking back along St. David Street from its junction with St. Mary Street is John Duncan's City Cycle Showrooms where customers had a wide choice including Duncan's own make of bicycle, the Royal Esk; the 'World's Best Value'. As well as acquiring a bike, shoppers in St. David Street could buy fish and game and, if they preferred to bag their own in the wild, there was a fishing tackle maker and gunsmith. People could also patronise a newsagent or licensed grocer, buy drapery or hats, visit a watchmaker or saddler and, when weariness set in, relax in one of James Gellatly's refreshment rooms or the Crown Inn.

One of the most imposing buildings in Brechin is the Mechanics Institute at the intersection of St. Mary Street and Church Street. It was built to the designs of Brechin-born architect John Henderson whose patron, Lord Panmure, provided the impetus and funding for the project. His coat of arms appears in a carved stone panel above the arched entrance. The institute was intended to accommodate the town's schools, public hall and library, and was begun in 1838 with the laying of the foundation stone as part of the burgh celebrations to mark the Coronation of Queen Victoria. In this picture, Church Street is seen on the right leading to High Street.

The remains of Maisondieu Chapel are situated in a vennel or lane of the same name and are seen on the left of this photo looking toward Market Street. Formerly associated with the cathedral, the Chapel was founded in the mid-13th century by William de Brechin and dedicated to the Virgin Mary. It was endowed with farmland to the north-west of the town. When its original function ceased, the building served as a residence and part of the structure was later converted into a stable, a role that was ended by a fire in 1825 in which a number of horses died. The structure that remains is of significant architectural interest.

In later years, when motor vehicles had become omnipresent, wheeling a barrow along a street would have been regarded as high risk, but it was evidently something people did about 1908 when this picture of Swan Street was taken. The picture looks back to St. David Street and the junction with High Street and Market Street. On the right, with two ornate lamp standards at the entrance, is the City Hall of 1883, which occupied the upper floor of the building with shops at ground level. Of these the most prominent in the picture is that of stationer and bookseller, J. T. Batchelor.

The practice of wheeling a barrow along Swan Street had apparently not died out by the mid 1920s when this picture was taken even 'though cars were more numerous. The view looks along the street from the High Street corner, with on the right a distinctive gabled building of about 1815. Further along the street were some big shops: Mrs Birse's ladies and gents clothier and hatter, another draper J. C. Robertson, seed merchant David Small, and Ferguson and Hood's ironmongery and oil merchants business – the oil being paraffin. Hairdresser and tobacconist David Spence sold his 'far-famed Dalhousie Mixture' pipe tobacco at his shop.

Brechin broke out of its medieval confines when the council acquired 'the Crofts' and adjacent ground to the north-east of the town. One of the former proprietors was Lord Panmure and so when a new thoroughfare extending from Swan Street was created in 1837 it was named Panmure Street. Lord Panmure was a staunch opponent of the Free Church when it broke away from the Established Church in 1843, but his son and heir had no such qualms and so the East Free Church, with its distinctive spire, was built on the corner with Southesk Street in 1855-56. The tall building closer to camera on the right of this picture, was built as the main post office in 1895 with the Clydesdale Bank moving from Swan Street to the adjacent site a few years later.

The former post office was located on the corner with Martin's Lane, which ran at right angles off Panmure Street before doglegging to run behind it on a parallel line. For many years it went no further until a new street, Eastbank, was created that formed a link between Panmure Street and Southesk Street to the east. It is seen here with mainly early 20th century semi-detached villas running down both sides of the narrow road in the days before parked cars made it even narrower. The curving wall in the right foreground corner of the picture indicates the sharp change of direction that takes the street to its junction with Southesk Street.

Eastbank joins Southesk Street directly opposite St Ninian's Square, the former site of the town's bow butts where men in medieval times were required to practise their archery skills in preparation for the day when they might be called to arms. Those times had faded into the past long before these cattle stopped, perhaps to slake their thirst at what appears to be a trough, while the humans could use the adjacent drinking fountain. The cattle seem unconcerned that there was a slaughterhouse nearby, so perhaps it too had been consigned to history by the time the picture was taken. The square was developed as a pleasant civic space at the turn of the 19th and 20th centuries.

The full shape of St Ninian's Square is seen in this picture used as a postcard in 1905. Across the background is the public library erected in 1891-93 to designs by architect James McLellan Fairley. In the foreground is an ornate drinking fountain made by sculptor, John Rhind. It was originally set up outside the Mechanics Institute in 1877, and moved to this site in 1895. An extraordinary sundial made by local mason James Tosh, that tells the time in 25 locations, sits in front of the library. A more recent addition is a statue, sculpted by Alan Herriot, of one of Brechin's most famous sons, Sir Robert Watson-Watt, whose work on the development of radar was vitally important to Britain's war effort. It was unveiled in September 2014 by Princess Anne, the Princess Royal.

The St Ninian's Square fountain is on the left hand edge of this picture from 1900 that shows St Ninian's Place, with the railway station beyond. Although the line opened in 1847/48 it wasn't the railway connection that the people of Brechin had hoped for. In the scramble to win Parliamentary approval for railway developments two companies, the Aberdeen Railway and the Perth-based Scottish Midland Junction Railway (SMJR) reached an understanding jointly to build a line through Strathmore on an agreed route, but things didn't work out as planned. At a very late stage in the process the Aberdeen Railway published their proposals, and because these by-passed Brechin they caused anger in the town and left the SMJR fuming at being blindsided.

Brechin had expected to enjoy the full advantages of its station being on a main line, but after the Aberdeen Railway's change of plan, found that it was at the end of a branch line from Bridge of Dun. The station was consequently a terminus with an attractive frontage and U-shaped arrangement of platforms as seen in this picture. In the 1860s, when many of the small Scottish railway companies were taken over by larger companies, the main Strathmore line became part of the big Glasgow-based Caledonian Railway although the Aberdeen Railway retained control of the Brechin branch. The 'Caley' finally bought it in 1894, opened branch lines to Forfar in 1895 and Edzell in 1896, and enlarged Brechin Station.

The station was flanked by sidings and sheds for handling goods traffic, always less glamorous, but arguably more important than passengers. In 1923 Britain's railway companies consolidated into the Big Four; the Caledonian became part of the London Midland and Scottish Railway (LMS) itself nationalised under British Railways in 1947. Brechin Station didn't last long after that; passenger services ceased in 1952 and freight in 1981. But having been by-passed in the early days, Brechin got the last laugh when a group of volunteers set about saving the branch line to Bridge of Dun as a heritage railway. Services began in 1993 and styled as the 'Caledonian Railway' the volunteers set about operating passenger trains and creating a tourist attraction for the town.

A tank locomotive is seen here standing outside the small local engine shed in 1936. She was built at the Caledonian Railway's huge engineering works at St. Rollox in Glasgow and entered service in November 1907. Her Caledonian number was 422, but when the LMS took over they gave her the number 15190 and British Railways would have given her the number 55190, but scrapped her instead. She had been in service for 40 years, testimony perhaps to her designer, the Caledonian's locomotive superintendent John Farquharson McIntosh. He was born at the Haughs of Kinnaird, just outside Brechin, started as an apprentice at Arbroath and rose through the ranks to become one of Scotland's great railway engineers.

Some of 'the Crofts' lands, that provided space for the town to expand in the 1830s, were acquired from the Southesk family whose Kinnaird Castle and estate lie to the south-east of Brechin, and so, like Panmure Street, a street was named in their honour. Southesk Street is seen here looking south from St. Ninian's Square (see page 23) close to where Eastbank joins on the right. Also on the right is the distinctive tower of the Gardiner Memorial Church on the corner with Damacre Road. Built to the designs of architect John James Burnet in 1896-98 it was named after the son of church benefactor the Rev. Alexander Gardner.

Linen manufacture was a big industry for Brechin. Initially weavers worked on their own handlooms but by the mid-19th century factories were being established, one of which was the large Denburn Works of D. & R. Duke situated at the southern end of Southesk Street, on the corner with Montrose Street. It is seen here in 1921 looking along Montrose Street toward the town centre. Initially set up as a handloom factory it was converted to operate power looms in 1863-64. It was a time of expansion in the industry when Brechin could boast of having a number of large works with a combined total of 539 looms employing 1,322 people. The Denburn Works ceased production in 1982 with the main part of the building later converted for housing.

The Denburn Works features prominently in this view, looking west toward the town centre from the vantage point of the Gas Works tower. Union Street, formerly known as Cadger Wynd, can be seen to the left of centre amongst the jumble of roofs. Gas works were never built in the most up-market parts of towns. They were smelly and unsightly, but provided a much-needed civic amenity, initially for lighting in streets, public buildings, shops and some private houses. Appliances for heating and cooking were developed later. Coal was baked in retorts to extract the gas, which was cleaned, purified and fed into large storage tanks ready to be piped to consumers. The process also created by-products like ammonia liquor, benzol and coke.

Formed in 1834, the Brechin Gas Company built its works off Witchden Road and as time went on upgraded the facility and increased capacity with new gasholders like the one shown here. In 1914, the company amalgamated with Edzell's gas company, closed its works and laid a six-mile-long main and storage capacity to supply that town with gas. The company also had a retail outlet for gas appliances at 29 High Street. The works achieved its highest ever output in the year to June 1947, but the following year the government brought forward the Gas Act to nationalise the industry.

Situated across Witchden Road from the gas works, the distinctive Maisondieu Church was built for the United Presbyterian congregation in 1890-92.

A gaggle of children has gathered for the photographer who took this picture of River Street leading down from Witchden Road in or before 1904. There are not many shops in evidence although the street did host quite a number including a boot and shoemaker, a dressmaker and milliner, dealers in bicycles, glass and china and a couple of grocers one of who styled himself as a potato merchant. A smithy was tucked in behind the houses on the right, as was the large Valley Linen Works. This was an industrial area where Brechin's first co-operative society was formed, the Upper and Nether Tenements Association – River Street was formerly known as the Nether Tenements.

River Street is one of those 'does what it says on the tin' street names as this view from the bridge shows. Looking impressively large here, the South Esk is a product of the beautiful Angus Glens. It starts as a mountain stream and as it rumbles and tumbles down Glen Clova is joined by the water of numerous burns. Sweeping past Cotachy the river is swelled by the outflow of neighbouring Glen Prosen and a few miles to the west of Brechin the Noran Water, coming out of Glen Ogil, adds to the main flow as it sweeps past Brechin and winds its way to the sea through Montrose Basin. It looks magnificent, it provided power for the town's early industries, but it was not always so benign.

The rain in early May 1913 was persistent and heavy, very heavy. Rivers rose and kept on rising as water running off the hills swelled the main channels into roaring torrents. Out in the countryside the South Esk swept sheep and newly-born lambs from the fields carrying them downstream. Tons of turnips were stripped from the ground, although men wielding pitchforks recovered a few cartloads of them. In Brechin, the river rose many feet above its normal level and didn't just overtop its banks, it poured over them as an unstoppable force inundating the lower part of the town. Hopes that the water would recede as quickly as it had risen were soon dispelled as the raging brown river kept on rising to reach its highest level for over 40 years causing part of a protective wall at the bridge to collapse.

River Street bore the brunt as water rose around the houses. People did their best, but lost the battle to prevent ground floor flats being flooded. Upstairs neighbours did what they could to help, while temporary refuge was provided in other houses and at the City Hall. The water did subside after a couple of days, but left mud-filled houses with forlorn strips of wallpaper hanging from dirt-stained interior walls. Outside, the street was strewn with boulders like the bed of a river, which for a time it had been. It was devastating for people who could ill-afford it, but it wasn't the first such flood nor the last and in 2015-16 Angus Council built major flood defences. Only a few years later, in October 2023, these proved inadequate when the river, mightily swollen by a major storm, overwhelmed the barrier and again inundated the largely redeveloped River Street and other riverside areas.

Rivers like the South Esk presented a significant barrier to people trying to move around the country and, in addition to that difficulty, early roads in Scotland were very poor, little better than packhorse tracks. Paradoxically some fine bridges were built, often prompted by churchmen and associated with the need for access to religious places. A bridge has therefore existed at Brechin for centuries with the earliest structure thought to have been of timber construction and in place as early as 1220. A two-arched stone bridge was built to replace it in the mid-15th century and engineer Alexander Stevens rebuilt the north arch in 1787. Known as the 'auld brig', it still carries the modern A933 to and from Arbroath.

At Bridgend there is a three-way intersection of River Street, Brechin Bridge and East Mill Road. The latter name refers to a mill driven by water drawn from the river by a weir that can be seen just below the bridge in the picture on the facing page. A spinning mill operated by the East Mills Spinning Company started operations in 1799 and quickly expanded. Steam power was introduced later, but the use of water for power continued. Imported flax was spun into a variety of yarns, bleached in adjacent fields and sent to factories throughout Angus and Fife. And the East Mill name was later used for a modern industrial estate that was also swamped by the October 2023 flood. Bridgend is seen here in a picture from about 1910 with the Brechin Laundry on the right.

Of the amenities that stretch across the north of the town, the public park was a particular source of civic pride when a portion was laid out to mark Queen Victoria's Diamond Jubilee in 1897 and then extended in 1903. It was funded by a gift from linen manufacturer Robert Duke of D. & R. Duke that paid for walks, embankments, garden seats, trees, flowers and shrubs, and the ornate cast iron fountain made by Walter Macfarlane's Saracen Foundry in Glasgow. The bandstand came later as did the war memorial, unveiled by Lady Dalhousie in December 1923 to commemorate the fallen of the First World War and subsequently augmented with names from the Second World War, Korea, Malaya, Kenya and Northern Ireland.

The ornate bandstand in the park was, like the fountain, made of cast iron at the Saracen Foundry in Glasgow. It was installed in 1908 and used regularly for performances by the Brechin City Band. They played there in June 1911 as part of the town's celebrations to mark the Coronation of King George V. The day started with a large flag, a gift from Lady Dalhousie, being unfurled at the High School. A service at the cathedral followed and a cricket match was played at Nursery Park. There was a gala for children at the public park in the afternoon, with sports including tug o' war and a variety of races. The band, seen here on the day, entertained the crowds from the bandstand and in the evening played music for dancing.

With a road and street named after it, Brechin Infirmary was the first health-care facility erected to the north of the town on a site adjacent to the public park. Funded as such institutions often were by subscription and donations, the foundation stone was laid in 1867 and the building opened a couple of years later. The following decade a poorhouse was erected behind the infirmary. Later, in the 1890s, in response to growing concerns over the treatment of infectious diseases, a hospital comprising separate wards for male and female patients and an administration block were erected. They are seen in this picture from around 1900 with the earlier infirmary visible behind, to the right. Still in use up to and after the setting up of the NHS in 1948, these buildings have since been superseded by a modern health centre.

R. Irvine, Trainer.　J. Melvin.　D. Glen.　W. Chapman.　W. Don.　A. Shand.　A. Skea.　R. Clift, Secy.
D. Easson.　R. Clark.　J. Lyon.　W. Graham.　H. Brown.
BRECHIN CITY F.C., 1907–08.

Brechin's name is known far and wide thanks to the existence of Brechin City Football Club. Founded in 1906 from two earlier clubs Brechin Harp and Brechin Hearts, it played in the Scottish League for many years, but dropped into the Highland League in 2021. The picture shows the table-topping team of 1907-08, with many of the men who beat Arbroath to win the Forfarshire Cup in season 1909/10, one of the club's proudest moments. The game, played at Dens Park, Dundee, saw Arbroath start strongly and have a goal disallowed for offside, but goals from Easson, Lyon and Clark swung the match in Brechin's favour. By way of celebration, James Lyon, father of the team captain, entertained the players to supper at the Star Hotel – no open-top bus parade through the streets in those days. The club moved to its new home ground at Glebe Park, with its famous hedge, in 1919.

The burgh council showed remarkable acumen in 1812 when it purchased an acre of land to add to the Common Den for the purpose of creating a nursery. A lease on the ground was offered by public roup, and the successful bidder was John Henderson who went on to create the Den Nursery, a feature of the northern side of town for many years. He and his sons continued to retake the lease for many subsequent years giving the town an income and providing people with fresh produce, seeds, cut flowers, roses, and shrubs. The nursery was also handily placed to make up wreaths and crosses for the neighbouring cemetery when it was established in the mid-19th century. The seven-arched bridge in the picture took the access road from Southesk Street across the den to the cemetery.

The North Port, not a harbour for ships but the name of one of the old town gateways, is seen here in a picture from about 1905. There was a North Port Brewery, but the name became more widely known after it was adopted for a distillery established in 1820 by the brothers, David, John and Alexander Guthrie. Originally it was known as Townhead Distillery, then Brechin Distillery and finally, to avoid confusion with the nearby rival, Glencadam Distillery, it became the North Port Distillery. Some of the distillery buildings occupied ground known as Gallow Hill, a name that remained in use for a street. Distilling ceased in the 1920s for a couple of years, again during the Second World War and finally when Distillers Company Limited closed the site in 1983.

Distilling was a significant industry for Brechin especially after the Glencadam Distillery, a rival to the North Port, was set up in 1825. One its early proprietors, David Scott, owned Springfield House a large Georgian mansion situated on the edge of town alongside Cookston Road. At that time the road ran north from the North Port area through largely open country, but this picture from the late 1930s, looking back down the road toward the town, shows that by that time some more modest dwellings had sprung up. More housing has since been built opposite the ones seen here and further north on both sides of the road. In 1895 an embankment and bridge were constructed in close proximity to Springfield House to carry the Brechin to Forfar Branch Railway over the road.

A 'sudden and severe' snowfall at the end of December 1908 blanketed the whole country. The north-east of Scotland was more severely affected than other areas with falls of up to eighteen inches and in places two feet recorded. The weight of snow brought down telephone lines, filled the railway cutting south of Montrose on the East Coast Main Line and blocked other railways and roads. Snowploughs got to work clearing the railway out from Brechin and local people with shovels did what they could to clear streets in the town but, as this picture of Latch Road, used as postcard in January 1909, indicates, they had a lot of digging to do.

About a mile to the north of the town, the burgh owned 33 acres of ground known as Trinity Muir (sometimes spelled Tarnty or Tarranty). It was used for many years as a trysting place – a place where a livestock market was held. There were four sales each year, in April, June, August and September, but the big one was June held over the course of three days. Sheep were sold on the Wednesday, cattle on Thursday and horses on the Friday. In between the sales the burgh let the market stance as pasturage and games of cricket were even played on it. The livestock sales were accompanied by sideshows and entertainments that over time morphed into a funfair with stalls and rides as seen in this picture from the 1920s or 30s. In the background is the reservoir of the Brechin Water Works opened in 1874.

In the 1830s and 40s the burgh sold ground from the market stance beside the then toll road. The new houses that were soon built on it became known as Trinity village, which is seen here in a picture from about 1930. The second last roadside building in the distance was originally a tollhouse. Beyond it is the former Trinity Muir Inn; in the turnpike road days, inns, tollgates and their respective activities often existed alongside each other. To modern minds these toll roads might seem ancient, but they formed the basis of the present-day road network, although the main A90 has relegated the old highway through Trinity to B-road status And Trinity has a new claim to fame as the home of Brechin Golf Club.

Two and a half miles north of Trinity is Stracathro, a place well known for many years to travellers to and from Aberdeen in need of a comfort stop and refreshment. The roadside services existed in close proximity to Stracathro Hospital, which was originally set up at the outbreak of the Second World War as an Emergency Medical Services hospital in the grounds of Stracathro House, a grand Georgian mansion built in 1827. It was used to accommodate hospital staff with the wards and other facilities in hut-like buildings. To begin with, injured civilians from bombed cities across Britain were brought for treatment, but soon military casualties also began to arrive. After the war the hospital was taken over by the NHS and staved off threats of closure to remain a valuable health care facility. The pictures show the house and hospital in 1949.